CINNAMON FIRE

CINNAMON
CINNAMON
CINNAMON
CINNAMON
CINNAMON
FIRE

poems by
Sheila Black

NEXT PAGE

Published by
Next Page Press
San Antonio, Texas
http://www.nextpage-press.com/

ISBN 978-1-7366721-8-1
Library of Congress Control Number: 2025950759

Book team:
Laura Van Prooyen, *director and editor*
Amber Morena, *book designer*

Cover art and part numbers by Sadie Clyne

"I wrote the word SUGAR on my palms.
I shall say what inordinate love is.
The moon rose itself up on its elbows and shook out its long hair."

—CONNIE VOISINE, "ANONYMOUS LYRIC"

Contents

ONE

TWO

CINNAMON FIRE

Recovery

My hard landing was different from yours.
I wound up in a trailer by a creek. Sunlight
crackled through a canyon, monkey flowers
sprouted beside clinking stones. Flames
of Indian paintbrush, plates of water
hemlock—so poisonous locals told me
campers had been known to die from using
their stems for tent posts or walking sticks,
skewers to roast marshmallows or meat.
All I could do was walk the trail each day—
an exposed skin in the world as you made your slow
journey from jail to rehab and back. Often, I
pictured you in the beige rooms with the orange
bucket chairs, chain-smoking cigarettes. I stared
into the crushed-foil water, songbirds bisected
the sky. My body like a stranger's—the usual
symptoms: hands shaking, a cramping. Recovery
takes time. That's what I was told, what I learned,
but something harder, too. How ill-equipped
I was in that shimmering landscape. And you and I—
what fresh pleasures we hungered, how easily we
mistook ourselves until we shrunk into our tired bodies.
You, drinking from the Styrofoam cups, leaning in
to hear all the sad stories—so much talking, talking.
The two of us locked in our tinny silence.
There was a dog—that's what I want to tell you,
the dog of the man who became my husband. He
walked beside me—mute and speckled, wet-nosed,
liquid-eyed, often racing ahead with a boundless
leaping as if he would never stop moving forward
into brightness. But each time he stopped as if there

were a thread that tied him, looping him back as if I
were the dumb stick to be fetched. What saves us?
That winter, a neighbor taught me how to dig myself
under in a blizzard. He promised the snow would
serve as a kind of blanket. "The trick to staying alive,"
he called it, but I thought only of the crystal-burn,
the dog who would find me, dig his black button
nose under the white so we might freeze together.

ONE

Predation

The gaze hushed by panes,
by pain, a glass streaked as though,
though not, by rain. Rule of I have seen
you here, you walk on a stair, you
turn away like the moon and gone.
Pure sky where the stars twitch—
bird-shadows or motes of dust
in a room where the chairs are stone.
Tensile and spun like glass
is through heat, liquid spirals—what
hardens, brittles. The self and the
meniscus between. The bird eyeing
the day-long butterfly, which flits as in
a delirium through the sugared flowers.

Elegy for Avenue B

Even the trees had jaundice
that winter. Waistlines thinned to
needles. Love, sex, death—anecdotes of
how fast they went. And the sweet
guile of the approach as we cozied
up to the bar, a gleaming wood
surface, razored, marked with
rings that interlocked. Bourbon, beer,
the sharp edge of a lime. I kicked
the leaves to the curbs, eyed the backs
of strangers. My fury had been
for nothing. I saw that now. Life
was colder, blood-gleam of spilled
pennies by a door, grit trail of
cigarettes, bottle caps we made into
trees along Tompkins Street Park.
The owner and his sons would be
dead by March. It happened that way—
out with a cold one week, in Saint
Vincent's the next. And love the
incarnadine. A whoosh of gasoline
on asphalt streets, horse races on
the television screen above the bar,
when the black mare broke her leg,
we lost our bet and stumbled out
to a milky oblivion of stars.

A List of What I Cannot Touch

the leather brace
the bedpan

the mirror's rippled surface, gold where the silver has been exposed

the pond
the carp with their huge blown mouths

their bodies that are almost clear

a list of what I cannot touch

pain child
ugly child

"God made her for a reason"

words I swallow. *I am not*, like the German
in the poet's throat

Ich, ich, ich

my mother brushes my hair, braids it with ribbons
I am a not-good-enough disguise

what I cannot touch

stiffness
pain

where a desire comes from to remake myself
in mirrors

chipped tooth, the tangled hair at the back of my head

the fact that if I concentrate, I can step straight

but my natural way is to be crooked

Alphaville

We played that game, moving from tenement
to drug deal—from the film by Goddard
where dismal project buildings
are refigured as galaxies, the rusty
Saab a rocket ship, a character's breathless
voiceover of traversing supernovas,
penetrating deep into uncharted space.
Purple twilight of November, the city
about to assume its diamond-hard coldness.
Halogen streetlights and steam from
manholes. Plexiglass windows thrown open
to knife winds off the Hudson. We never knew
what the men on the stoop were thinking.
The one from the building next door who
played fretfully with his knife—spinning it
on its point. His buddies with their repeat
performances of "waterfall of cards,"
games of dice, and three card monte. The girls
who moved through as if underwater. Call
our lives a drowning, hands lifted as if
to pull in or ward off. Seaweed and barnacles,
galactic dust swirled around skyscrapers. We
walked Amsterdam to Columbus and back,
a chemical warmth, sudden lapse into liquid
space. Who can say how far we were going?
Yards and light years, such a falling
and falling inside. At the grill of the bagel
bakery at 5:00 am, we could see the women
with the white handkerchiefs tied around
their heads loading heavy trays on silver carts.
You never even wanted to eat, but we passed
our cash through the bullet-proof window.
Bread from solar ovens bloomed in our hands.

Cento for Us

Your word is echo, *mine is unfold*.
Red in the flawless blue of the sky.

The moon stands up in darkness.
What are you thinking about?

Here is our street   shaky.

Little evening, I walk across the stone
bridge, helloing the future.

Hard Candy

That antic grief—I miss it,
when any plaza was poured concrete multiplied

to infinity, anywhere you weren't the worst kind of
party, where the drinks are water mostly

made sour by lime, and someone talks about condos
or Salesforce or the game where you shoot

people in cars and the cars crash and burn, a theatre
of fires along roadsides. What was the song,

the one I played so continually you howled,
a song that only became unbearable when you

were forced to listen to it by the girl in gray sweats,
her platinum dyed hair, hand curling

upward like a baby bird for a cigarette. The song had
something to do with a car and burning

but the trick was the singer sang it as if from underwater,
emotionally speaking—that haze, that shimmer,

that trick of swallowing pain. I'm scared I'll never master it
or get used to being ghosted by you—awful

rehearsal dinner for final parting or that we come
to love with such a feeling of having been always lonely.

All the more reason to scar, to paint over, to mar,
to eat all the double chocolate with fudge ripple and nuts

it really doesn't need crammed in the little container
just because they can.

Aubade for Longing

There are still songs to be sung on the other
side of the human.

Even as paradise turns to winter,
the whales

disappear with their soundings, absence stitches
the sea.

Infinitesimal spaces in my brain grow and split—
sieve of snowflake, shadowbox,

saint's finger-bone. A car
careens a curve, a radio throbs in a distant room,

a song about what stops.

And what are you but this flicker inside me
for which I invent a season,

a beach front hotel, an opera.

Flux of light in a city I have not visited
in years,

pavement

that bears our fleeting mark.
Posters peeling and you, you, you,

a silence that swoops through,
arguing endlessly against the notion

of silence.

Lontaine

1.

In those days, I often walked

without direction, not infrequently seized by

a longing to fling myself

down to the earth, to dig a hole & pour my voice in.

Afraid, at times, I might start hugging the trees—

blood sister of cherry, moon-bark of aspen,

Often, I wondered at my purpose—

this dogged sorrow, which had taught me so little,

until I understood I was struggling to construct myself around

an absence:

what-I-desired-and-could-not-will-to-be.

2.

When autumn came, the pain attenuated to almost-pleasure:

the world now limpid, my mirror—

pale grass, high wind, bruise clouds drifting over,

even the somehow tortured-looking shapes of the junipers.

Ice filled the space behind my eyes. I believed I had never

seen each object in the world so clearly

or understood what desert and plain and forest might mean,

those spaces where people still enter

as alien, outside the range of hearth or village, town or strip-mall,

far from creature comfort.

3.

Rain pelted and turned to hail.

Icicles coalesced along the edges of the buildings.

One morning the car refused to start.

I walked until my fingers were blue, and I was afraid to look at my toes,

like icefish, deep under a lake, the fact that they freeze

in place, sometimes years.

4.

You left on a journey and came back

tanned and speaking loudly. I pretended not to notice

the precise manner of you not noticing me.

Winter crackled inside, a hunger for eternity,

until I believed I understood even the trees in ice,

the meekness of lawns, the grasses' inexorable stiffening,

believed I would choose to stay awake through any operation,

which was why I watched you, just watched you,

regardless of the pain it caused me,

so long had I sought to enter the realm of pure feeling.

Hurt Magic

It lived in the words we whispered
by the side of the bar, where people played pool,
or got so drunk they shouted every word
or grew mad or sad for no reason.
You told me a story about a Persian king
who built a garden of stone
to please the woman he loved. Stones, diamonds,
—the trees of jeweled fruit,
which, of course, left the problem
of nothing to eat. The image is what
makes us lonelier—I believe this. For years,
I carried your story like a boxwood
reliquary sealed inside my chest. Later,
you told me a different story about
your time in the service—the day you
found a dead horse with a blue scarf
wrapped around its neck, early morning,
nestled in a field of stones. Whose horse?
You saw a girl howling at the sky. You saw
an old man who spat on the ground as you passed.
The scarf was silk and would have had
some value. Embroidery around its
edges, white lilies, contrasting with the flies
that already covered the horse's eyes.
Once I gifted you a bottle of expensive liquor, you broke
the neck and drank it straight from the jagged
glass. We both knew how to picture moonlight
in a stone garden, how it deflects from the pale
polished marble, the granite drinks it in
fathoms at a time.

Slow Alphabet of Rain

We haven't had any. I keep watching the sky—
any puff of wind. I pity the dates
from the date palm, which are so pale
they look like monstrous almonds, speckling
the sidewalk besides a grackle that
is just sitting there, which makes me think
it must be sick. The woman who disappeared
was not a stranger—she'd grown up here,
and she loved the arms of the saguaro
because they reach up like human beings.
She called herself a "Pilgrim of Silence"
whatever that means. It took them days to find
her—up against a thin feathery palo verde,
which should have provided enough
shade, but didn't. Rain, which has become in my
lexicon equivalent to longing, which is
to say to memory. That night on
East 7th Street you told me you would die
soon, but you were laughing, and it was obvious
you didn't believe it, and neither did I. One
thing you said was true—it would be like
simply stepping off, which it was for you,
"the suffering of the body and then it stops."
But we loved our suffering—every greasy
diner and the onions on the grill, and the mist
in winter that rose up, radiators steaming,
the mass of bodies from the bald maws
of the subway gates, people with
fingerless gloves and bruises, and the voices
shouting about the paper. I used to put out

my hands just to feel the engine of the-so
-many lives. *Pilgrim of Noise.* Here, when I
look at the sun I feel as if I am looking into
my love which burned too hot with fear
to be of any use to anyone. The rain that touched
us, equally—your hair plastered against your
your forehead, mine swinging through the air,
that spring of so much rain moss inched
even the sidewalks; inside every green
another green unfurling.

Aubade for the City that Never Sleeps

The buildings half-knocked down
are still inhabited by women
who beat the rugs in the morning
with brooms, who peel the bananas
with a wrist flick that speaks
of necessity and its hard blood taste,
a blooming at the back of the tongue.
Peonies explode from a store front:
Carmine, acid yellow, the tender white
of oblivion. What is the world but a mouth
that demands feeding? Love, the secret
dew folded inside the envelope
of a leaf battered by the many feet
walking across the unspeakable bridge
that leads to the tunnel of the twelve-hour
journey, Imagine a people who refuse
to believe in death, choosing instead
to valorize the singular story of each
footfall. Here is where the burning
occurs. Morning, you lift your dark cup,
and we drink.

The Home Front

I watched the way you held your wrists
as if expecting some heavy gift—
a basket of bread that sounds
hollow when you tap on it, golden
and feathered on the tongue, a split plum
too juicy for the thin skin to hold it in.
Once you said, "I didn't know
anyone who died." I thought you
were telling me you were lucky, but
you were only saying you didn't know
anyone you'd killed. Mornings, you
turned your back to me, cupping
a coffee mug. You liked to look at trains,
you liked to watch the blackbirds rise
from the onion fields at the edge of town,
half in love with how they held
themselves together, yet so apart.
I could already see the time I wouldn't
know you anymore, when I'd mistake
your back for the back of a different man,
a memory of you like a coin
at the bottom of a fountain covered
in moss. Knew what I would keep—
an image of red birds in heavy snow,
pecking the ground for a seed that skitters,
just out of reach. Down by the river
a person flapping their arms in blue light.

Season

We scooped up a few grains,
the yard a deep green knife in the morning.
Minty tomatoes on their stakes,
the high sound of insect legs flexing together.
We rubbed the seeds in our hands
to watch them fall to dust as children do,
tearing the leaves from every plant
to put *this this this* in our mouths.

At Times Presence Is a Kind of Wound

It's easy to be disquieted by grief,
how the dead put bread in the mouth,

leave marks on stones
that tell you which turn you should make

on a dirt road on which you can see
traces of other feet.

At times presence is a kind of wound—
to sit under the catalpa tree

in the blue-black noon and hear
the buzzing of insect legs.

Where were you meant to go? The dead don't answer,
but leave divinations, clues.

Each time you uncover a new fork,
it is as if they are there waiting to say,

"We told you so." For a long time, I couldn't
look at photos of you, your being there

so much like my being here. I did not
know I'd loved your face so gravely—

like a listener able to hear the fluttering in your
chest, your face a movie screen

with meanings projected across it. I believed
I had lived inside your skin

at least a little, lived a while inside all that's
gone, nudging up against it at the kitchen

counter as I poured my coffee and looked
out at my ragged yard in the blue hour

before bright sun and work again.

Heartbreak

In the card, the figure is alone
facing three spilled cups

while behind her abundant goblets
brim and froth, but she does not notice.

A river, a mountain, but flat and
inimical as though it would take her

decades to reach them. I swallowed your
name as if by hiding a word

I could escape the pain. Now
I speak in a tangle of frogspawn

mixed with half-dead flowers—messy
decaying things, a bitterness

when I drink the clearest water.
I loved the gamble—to stake

so much of myself on something like
a walk in the park—like the coming

of an ice storm when, out of the blue,
the trees turn to knives, each glittered

in strangeness—vivid, also solitary,
a little desperate,

like a woman in a Greyhound station
begging money for a ticket anywhere.

I forgot that, as ice breaks, even the sharpest
desire can break,

leaving one person holding the shards.
The figure with her spilled goblets. She should

bend over and pick them up, but this is art
where nothing happens—

Aubade for Inordinate Love

You hurt me more than anyone,
and I still mistake this hurt for love:
great ghost of a thing like the manta
ray I once swam beside for a whole
quarter mile, astonished it could be so
slender yet alive—a kind of cloud
in the water, a shape that made
me think that this must be what is
meant by soul, surface tuned to
the world so acutely that close as it
came it never brushed against me.
The ones who keep them in aquariums
claim they are like dogs, attuned
to our griefs and rages, even allowing
themselves to be stroked, rolling
over to show their pale-gray flanged
bellies. The one that followed me was twelve
feet across—yet I could not feel afraid.
We live alone in so much water,
and it appeared to only want to play.
When we reached the surf, it turned
sideways and vanished. I never saw
it again, though I looked. Love
is like that, gaining traction from
knowing when to withdraw, nothing
to be done but apprehend its distances,
blue light on far waves.

Arroyo Seco

The cottonwoods are thinking again about creek bed
in March, when the snowmelt trickles, then rushes,
and the thickness of caliche, and the treachery of holding
anything long enough in this place, especially water.
How the earth will form a bed around whatever lies
in it long enough, and you can read the signs if you stay
alert, and the vultures whose job is to keep the dead moving,
so that fire can start up again and lick its way across
the stands of the pines and stir new forests to life
from the mats of last year's leaves. The stoneflies are thinking
about home, and the effort it takes to build a tiny wall of
spit and pebble, and how soon their lace wings shrivel,
and how long their little houses sit empty, making home
only for the wind. The girl is thinking about virga and
that the name sounds like *viga*, like the ones that hold up
the heavy adobe roof of her low-ceilinged house, and how
she would prefer to be like the ghost rain, the walking rain,
that synonym for longing: what falls and never touches down.
The only story a child learns: to fly is to burn into the sun.

Amaryllidaceae

1.

In my dream state of New Mexico, the onion
fields sing and breathe. They know

how to discard a skin without regret,
but also, how to make beauty.

In my dream state,
I hand you armfuls of onions that desiccate

in the clear, clear desert air. They resemble
the wings of moths

or translucent birds. They fly through the hot
wind.

They land at our feet.

2.

I never told you I loved you.

I find it amusing in a bitter-almond way,
the elaborate prohibitions I set

around these words that still carve

a hole in me, bone-smooth, bone-dry,

filled with onion-wings.

3.

Our dream state was border-uncomfortable.

Sometimes I was your stalker.
Sometimes you almost needed me.

I misinterpreted every word you said
or spent fretful hours

transcribing, revising. This was the madness

that Sophocles found age redeemed him from.

What is the inscription for loving what doesn't
love you back?

4.

Lessons of distance. Lessons of time versus space.
Lessons of relative weight.

I am planting onions. Their flowers resemble
lilum, resemble daffodils,

resemble narcissus stripped back to
pure form,

as Narcissus himself was stripped.
What could be more horrible than to find

you love only yourself?

The bulb in the ground, the bloom
flavorless,

but nevertheless edible.

5.

In my dream state of New Mexico, I cover
myself with onion flowers.

I know these will not last.

I know the truth is the hollow my body makes in this red earth.

On this bare red hill where I never

told you what I was most possessed
to say.

6.

Now the November fields,
rust of the used world.

Do you remember how the tall grasses bleach as they die?

Nothing else resembles that bleach-shine, not gold
but the ghost of what gold is—

a rising. We want most love—

what actually happened.

Two

The Amaryllis Surprises Me Again

We cook brown rice and black beans,
eat them with diced fresh
tomatoes from the garden. A pleasure
in growing old, though we grow
more forgotten, tangled like roots.
Your thin ankles under the flannel
robe in the mornings when you
stand like God over the coffee maker,
measuring. Sitting on the back stoop,
we drink out of the brownware
mugs. Much of the garden we fail
to keep alive in the changing
climate. Sometimes a week of rain,
and the whole world greens
again. I am never prepared
for when this happens—the amaryllis
on my kitchen windowsill dies
away every year until I swear
there is nothing left of it.
What is the secret inside the heavy bulb?
A sprinkle of water, a damp heat.
The flower springs up almost as
big as my face, and red, the red
of arterial, a kind of tear in the air.
Here is my life. You, what I was given.

Everywhere and Nowhere at the Same Time

It is a race against the sun. I think of you as I
pace the hot yard, trying to resurrect the pepper
plant, begging it with my artificial rain to unfurl
its yellowing leaves. It is a race against the moon—
that moment of stepping into dark as into
ocean, believing for the span of a few breaths
there is no boundary here. Your face floats in stars,
emerges from an indeterminate mass of
cloud. This is what it is to be ghosted. I know
what comes back is my own echo; yet, how can it not
be blended in some way with what you were? I
watch two leaves emerge from the dry earth,
a tiny fleck of green, and how it divides, divides.
Every day, acute miracles of becoming—shadows
folding up their umbrellas to walk home.

August

My heart feels so still. Only the grackles
and finches outside on the deck,
morning's face, and to watch it
arrive a little later each day. Inside
for months, we view the world through
a scrim: bluish dragonfly,
carmine bougainvillea that sprouts
as if trying to devour the fence.
I can see stars even as the sky lightens,
their peculiar fixity—a burning
that never stops or at least not in any
time I can follow. You've stocked
the house again—the gluten-free bread,
the big jars of peanut butter and honey,
a bag of slightly wizened apples.
I should notice more the care you
take—middle-of-the-night trips
to the store to get me cough syrup
or ice cream. Your constancy.
The wind shifts, leaves lift, rustle.
Who will remember our traceless
civilization—rituals of walking the dog,
wasting Sundays with television?
Deeper things only you and I saw:
green herons colonizing the cedar,
hunting the neighbor's kittens,
our child dying at birth, then jolted
back to life, infused with blood from a chilled
storeroom. I want to believe in a God
that is simply the record of all things
as a leaf is veined or a stone pocked
with the marks of each ice-age, each
summer-of-all-the-forests-burning.

The Earth

What can I tell her over breakfast when she says
her son suffers from madness, and because there
is no mental health, he has ended up in jail,
and she is relieved, because at least he might
be safe there or he might get to see the doctor.
We are eating egg-white omelets, we are counting
carbs. We are buttoning ourselves in our clean dresses
and high-heeled shoes in order to bring home the bacon,
doing what we need to do and "It is what it is."
Her granddaughter and daughter are living with her
in the one bedroom. Nights, the daughter lounges by
the pool, looking at her phone, while she teaches the child
to plant seeds in a flower bed she feels bad she does not own.
She tells me she cried in the car coming here; she did not know
me then. She thought we would be talking to each other
the whole time about what we are selling, what
the other might buy, but somehow we left that behind
over the toast with the tiny pots of strawberry jam.
Who can explain all this luxury, all this despair?
Or how we all hold our secret shames so close
and gloss our lips with "Cinnamon Fire" as if that were
some legitimate form of protection. Cinnamon Fire!
She just turned fifty. I tell her wait ten years—you
won't know more, but you will get closer to forgiving
because it is all happening on a wheel that spins
so fast. Why not stop to look at the pink flowers
you've planted with your granddaughter? Why not feel
your bare toes in the good wet earth? We play with the crusts
on our plates. The waitress takes the coffee away. We
are strangers again, each carrying our lonely fear
our children won't find their way, wishing for them

some inner logic—sacred trust of earth and self, that exists
for each of us so far within, so far under the skin, we
can't even begin to say what it is made of, it merely is,
poised between love and grief: the blue space we call wonder,
which is merely the dew on the grass, the shadow the sun
makes as it rolls over the vast skin of the Earth.

Unrequited

I worked in an office with a window that looked out
over a sycamore. My lovelorn boss popped Xanax
over lunch hour. Once I found her asleep under
her desk. Her stockinged feet sticking out from under
her rolling chair made me think she might be
dead. I remember her weeping face, twin
to my own. How I hated living in the same spaces
I knew you walked through—a feeling like a scent
in the air I was always missing. I fixated on the bark
of the sycamore, its extravagant peeling, a patterning
of purple, pumpkin, aura of scar. Often, I stole
a bit to worry in my fingers—smooth and cool,
dry and somehow private. I mapped and remapped
our geometries, wanted to understand every elective
affinity—what drives subatomic particles towards one
another across vast swatches of space? My boss and I
went out for margaritas often. I admired her raucous laugh.
Her ex-husband worked on the floor above. She
called him out over the office listserv, suggesting
instead of posting moronic truisms about positive
work culture, why not stop being a lying, cheating skank?
They fired her. After, we still met for chips and salsa,
and lots of tequila. She got a job driving a firetruck,
taught herself to skydive. Said it woke her up
to plummet down like a stone—almost forgetting
to pull the cord, but at the last moment hoisted
as if by wings. I liked this image of her—arms
akimbo, her haloed hair. But mostly I liked
how she spoke of her ex with such forthrightness.
Her heart had been shattered, and she was not
afraid to wear it. I was the exact opposite.

I traced designs of Orion in notebooks—a hunter
frozen in lost pursuit. What stars would he ever catch
up there in the green-black dark? I considered
the virus of love, implacable force giving off
its half-life light—came to see it as a toxin, which I
tried to leach out by hugging the sycamore
all through that winter as it shed its leaves, its bark
in long delicate curls across the hard-packed dirt.

Letter in Spring

Needless to say, I am still rooting
for the orange tree to come back,
even though its thin dead twigs, frozen
in our unexpected polar-vortex freeze
seem to promise otherwise. I'm
convinced I will run into you
along the Riverwalk or under the oaks,
and we will be able to pick up
the thread as if it never broke. I'm
holding out hope that my husband's
cloud of pessimism will abruptly lift,
and he will bring me lilies, armfuls
of them, for the Easter in which we
will all rise up as out of our graves to live
doubly so. I'm telling you—him—come out
here. Look at the train tracks, and the
tender shape of the yellow dog, who has
lived here wild, but begging when she
needs to, longer than us even. Look at
the cardinals, the pair of them, how they
scoot a little impatiently from branch
to chicken-wire fence and back. Do you think
they are arguing over whether to stay—
why this yard and not the one next door?
Do you think, like us, they have learned
to love our mutilated mountain laurel,
half-dead bougainvillea, this mighty
orange tree, now a ghost, which year
after year managed, despite its diminutive
size, to yield so many, such oranges?
My husband has his eyes to the binoculars.

He is telling me he heard owls again
last night. Sometimes we feel as distant
as continents but really we are like the
ocean beneath, full of large animals sending
signals across cold blue waters.

Solstice

Blood on snow is the cardinal in the yard.
The sudden deep freeze.
A glitter.
Listen!
Here we are among the gloved.
No wings.
Only the slow blades which break away
into the snow-melt water.
Between two junipers, a child blinks
into the glass of the moon.
I do not dare disturb the water.
I listen as she breathes, aware of nothing
outside the circle of light that
is moon and moon child.
A silence ripples and reaches me.
How alone we are.

Elegy with Orion

I don't believe in the stars exactly or the man
who told me my palm was cut in two
by "love troubles," but I look to Orion every time I
tilt my head skyward this time of year—
days shortening, the promise of pure winter—
brother, hunter, rapist—murdered
by Artemis for his unspeakable crimes.
There he is eternally chasing the stag with his shining quiver.
Here are the stars tonight—such cunning fairy lights,
but draw closer, and they are maws of fire
swallowing whatever would breathe beside them.
I have loved you best in glimmers.
I don't know what I would do with you if I had you.
Yet I shadow you as Orion shadows me,
a kind of *imago* spelling out the ancient grief of
how bad a person can be and still be beloved.
The Greeks were smarter than we are about such things.
They knew longing makes you cruel, knew
what you love can destroy you. Remember
that night we sat in a bar trading stories—
childhood favorites, ending on *The Snow Queen*.
Her splinter enters the boy's eye, and the girl
travels to find him. Only her tears will make
the world beautiful again. I loved that story once,
but now I think it as troubling as the hunter,
the good brother, terrible guest, who pillages
where he can. See how even now
he circles home.

Fever

What I most want is a different kind of sentence,
one that admits a stillness:
The peacock feather—

that lucid
blue-green eye that is not an eye
no matter how many times we call it one.

What was it you said to me? —a few words, garbled—
but something in your hands,

a feeling as if

your hands were bleeding, and I
had neglected to see.

In those days, we could try on the costumes of the war
in the charity shops at the far ends of the boulevards.

The sedge-green jackets with ornate brass buttons,
often an eagle or a man's face.

You said they drilled into his skull but wanted him
to stay alive (the shapes of the words

in your mouth)—

I want the feeling of the bread we bought,
of peeling circus posters outside Penn Station.

All that has left the world. I can change
how I speak or how I piece together

the words or
I believe I can change,

and sometimes I believe
the words will cut in and deepen—other times

they are mere white noise,
no more or less than leaves on trees,

What it would be to uncover
the stillness behind? *Febrile* was

the word I used when sweat sheened your face or
you put out your hands to show me how

they would not stay still.

The Coming World

I watch tar slide off a roof. I think of
going to get a cold beer. Someone
left two cookies to melt on a black plastic
plate beside a fountain whose water
appears unnaturally blue. We, too, were
unnatural. I speak to you even though you
are not here. Remember when we walked
the hot acequias, taking shelter
in thickets of bamboo, not native,
but planted there, and taking root.
They formed tiny forests of slight cool,
and in those narrow green spaces it was possible
to believe the coming world might be ours
after all. Now I am old, a person no one
notices, which in the stakes of the world,
feels a puny sacrifice. The stakes which
are splintering so the young woman
in the office next to mine jabs her eyes
with her fists and says, "I know I'm crazy, but
when I can't sleep, I feel my own heart
in my mouth, and it is bleeding."
On the hot long walk, I ask imaginary you
what you think of this. I ask you in this poem,
knowing full well— We go on. We get lonelier,
give up even those who feel as necessary to us
as salt. I sit on a bench under a concrete
statue of a palm with the young woman,
describe for her each greening desert thing:
datura, agave, yucca, creosote, saguaro,
the way each spring blossom arrives out of
nowhere, disappears just as abruptly.

Medea Talks About Our Stars

I tell her, "Listen, I was always timid."
"Not timid," she says, "ashamed."

I look at her in her ragged red dress,
her bare feet and cracked toes,

her eyes so ravenous I look away,
but even when I brush past,

even when I mutter, "You don't understand,"
she clings to me like the smoke

of a charred meat—goat maybe—roasted
in a pit with branches of oregano

burning their green into the blackened bits of wood
left on the ground.

"Watch my lips," she says,
"No safety,"

and I think of how in the night I have hugged myself,
so lonely I felt like a blade of the moon,

some sort of chipped metal, a mezzaluna
over a board of onion

skins and tears. All she would like me to do
is sit down with her at a table

and drink stewed tea in the bleached morning.
All she cares about is that I acknowledge

the brutal stars of love—the ways we are nothing
without their daggers, breathing as we do

so briefly under their long dead lights.

Cherries

What life would I have had
if I had not pulled back out of fear,
if you had not died?
I am pitting cherries for pie,
digging the little tool inside
to pull out the hard stone,
eating as many as I pit—their slight
musky taste, sugar but with an edge.
My husband, who never knew
you, or even much about you,
once drove me through orchards
of them, planted along Flathead Lake.
The lake, a desert sky color in that
Northern plain, made me think of
you. You once worked on a project
to seed clouds. The logic so simple,
you said—if water falls, a world
greens. If water falls—is it forever
the same water? My bowl of hollow
cherries waits. Life, like a painting
composed of such random
associations. That day along
Flathead Lake was beautiful. We
stopped and paid a man five dollars
to pick a bucket of his cherries,
our lips and hands stained when we
pulled over later to get a motel in
Spokane. A professor I had back then,
a generous man, had a place on an
island in the middle of the lake,
which he called in conversation

"The eye of the sky in the center of the
world," an awkward way of saying
the place had echoes. He died there,
two years after, trying to leave the cabin
too late in the season, he and his wife
plunged into the glacial waters. The police,
at first, suspected murder-suicide,
then they found the bodies of their dogs,
two golden retrievers, who'd capsized
the boat, the theory went, by jumping
in from the shore. Wild. Unaccountable,
the way the unpredictable rips out
your heart. Your heart just stopped. I
eat a fistful of cherries. Spit out the pits
in my palm. I do this kind of thing
habitually, without thinking.

Aubade for Losing

It's old the sadness
that we don't know how to keep anything, the words

once like birds now fall like leaves snipped from a
tree by winter.

Pain with her long needles. Silence with her smooth mask.

A room without windows or door,
but bone-pale from a light you can't see

as if whatever made us—whatever we were made from—
contains a necessary rupture.

What a thing to be locked in a single body,

one hand, then the other, trying to turn themselves
into birds.

End of Day, "Nightscape V."
by Louise Nevelson

Build a city in a box or as a kind of
machine and paint all the pieces for night.

Burnish the wood to a metallic gleam
until all the city shines.

Turn out the light and show us the screen
on which we project whatever we dream.

Build a city in a box, an instrument, a scene
to show us our lungs are as one.

Fretwork of notes or gears that can play
like the inside of a piano or a tempered violin.

Make a city in a box full of memory drawers,
each one with a different relic inside.

Shapes that falter, shapes that fill, round holes
in square pegs—tiny boxes of still.

Make a city of beds and invite us to sleep.
Invite us to remember, invite us to dream.

Planed wood, painted ebony plain,
plain wood that reminds us of furniture

we left—grandmother's closet, uncle's
armoire—emptied of whatever they might

or must have contained. How many
rooms can we recover in the City of Night,

space of secrets, loss and delight? And how
we are linked, and how each our own,

and how every container contains itself alone.
City of Numbers, City of Dread,

City Abandoned Except in One's Head—
"Describe the Night," she asks as in a dream

and answers with boxes, and beds, and screens,
glazed as if by wind or rain, until the wood glitters

like porcelain. Trellis that quiets even the air.
City of Longing which is no longer there

Dawn Chorus

Those years the bed felt like a boat,
and our limbs pressed against the limbs
of sick children, the hair in the mouth,
the stumbling—floral, immense, down the hall
for the sticky, sickly cherry-flavored medicine.
One coughed, then another, one turned
into a dream, which made them moan in terror.
And the awake dry-mouthed mother who
believes/has learned the dream is merely life.
But what joy in that wide bed, the birds in their
dawn chorus, the trickster ones who sang
in the middle of the night as if to say moon
is sun, time is not or would not ever be
as it had been. An owl coughs from a tree.
A child coughs back. Later we would think
we had thought this forever—our bodies tied
to them as if by thin moonlight threads,
but it was only a season, a rotation. The
swallows' nests left behind each year to
crumble into dust, littering the back porch
with their intricate broken weaving.

Afterlife

An abundance—like dandelion fluff
filling the spaces.

To believe you are somewhere
eating vanilla ice cream, engaged in your quixotic

celebration of wonder—how about those
squirrels that run across

the phone lines, careless, consuming a single
bite of pear and tossing it away? Or that time snow

fell in May, and we woke to trackless alleys,
white crystals making the air flicker

as if alive, as if the flanks of a great horse—
galloping into the blue powders of day.

I unpack my chests of memory.
I want their humbleness—

the taste of roast meat, sheets folded in
a drawer, the privilege of ordinary time,

which hung on us like clothes we did
not know how to wear.

How We Live

He knows where the owls are. I don't until
he shows me, and when he does, we
watch the parents feeding the children,
going out to savage what they can,
and then the sweet motion of the tiny
feathered throats. We hold the binoculars
to our eyes as you might hold the words
of a catechism. We recognize what
we see, yet cannot forget the curled blue
mouse bodies. The little owls' eyes shine,
not like the moon, but like the jittery
neon signs along our local highway,
which shiver at such a rate they make
our city seem larger, stranger than it is.
Tell us how we must live, we ask the flat
disk of a moon we know will never answer.
The question still feels important. Another day,
another raptor—this time the caracara, two
of them, hooded-eyed, perched on telephone
poles above a cinderblock ranch where a gray
tabby has crept onto the lawn to die after being
struck by a car. The birds lift their wings—oh
span of great distance. *Here we are.*

Medea by the Water's Edge

What she discovered at the edge:
how easily even a rock face

can be battered—to stand naked,
sluiced through,

all boundaries irrelevant.

So much water, water,
the sensation of becoming all motion.

She longed like any lover
for the moment to be a wave

and to not be a wave,
impossible to keep her desire

knife-sharp, just as it was.

Shivering in the scum of tides,
she gazed ahead.

Ruin where she was headed.
She took a breath and dived in.

She would learn to live in a style of drowning,

to rise from oceans, to be the one
who haunted the future by consuming

whatever she was given.

Wintering

In my room overlooking the treetops, I spy
the cardinal and his smaller mate
moving over leafless branches.
It wasn't for you I wanted to burn down
my life, but the idea of you, like a stick
of incense giving up its vanilla, its patchouli,
freezing something not meant
to be frozen. *Minor blue-violet,*
summer dusk. Outside a tree-of-heaven
tilts skyward, its acrid, awkward
blossoms, below the soil a monster
of inter-connected roots. To hold what
is fleeting next to what will last
or what refuses to be destroyed.
Tree-of-heaven, also known as knotweed,
able to spring back from the slightest live
stalk. I don't know what to make
of such survival—when young it was
easy to see pain as merely a means
of pushing through, to believe in abundance.
I have a memory of the dusty
vaulted ceiling of the narrow church
we used to visit, named for San Ysidro,
patron saint of farmers, rain prayers.
Being a gardener, the saint knows death
to his fingertips, the practice of planting,
planting, seeing nothing flower.
Tonight, two small red birds lift off from
the bare branches of the dying laurel,
follow each another all though morning.

Walking the Neighborhood

A few things I've learned—when a tree erupts
in bird noise, a predator is near.
The hawks prefer the higher branches, often
just sit—a quarter of an hour even,
waiting their moment, and then it comes,
gorgeous flare—feathers unreeling,
scalloped, dark, edged with pale cutlasses,
crescent moons. We pass a dead crow beset
with snails—surreal and grotesque,
a muffled bird shape. Who knew
snails could get so ravenous? Even
the local pond I used to think of as calming
erupts when I toss my crumbs across it
—turtles, eels, fish whose fins
though small, appear razor-tough
all of them eating—the bread, each other.
And the sky is so summer blue, a pool one might
fall headlong into—indigo, cloud.
What do our words do but dice the world into pieces?
I think this, dragging my lame leg, noticing how
a few others stare at me—that calm hostile stare
that seems to say, "you should not be here,
you who are not like us."
The speed of the caracara as it descends—I've
watched it this week two or three times,
savage and beautiful or beautiful
and savage. I cannot decide which.
Am I the mouse running across the

vacant lot—that desperate body
possessed by the wings which
shadow it? And the caracara—
its eyes level, appears
entirely possessed by sky.

I Played for You on My Instrument of Longing

and the threads cut my fingers, and I reveled in the streaks,
the reverberations that would drive me

high up into the tree. I stood straight as a flower,
a hurt opening as if to make me

a bride of sky. *Unrequited* and its muzzy
infinities—like the view of clouds out an airplane window.

This morning a flock of geese arrow a horizon of snow,
knotted together as if murmuring endearments.

I learned from you the prison of being alone while thinking
only of another.

The geese look down at the land they're leaving.
And nothing holds them but air.

Note

In "Cento for Us," the lines in this cento come from Melissa Kwasny's poem "Clairvoyance," and Jenny Browne's poem "Dear Stranger."

Acknowledgements

Grateful acknowledgement is made to the following publications where versions of these poems first appeared:

Academy of American Poets Poem-a-Day: "The Earth"

Asheville Poetry Review: "The Amaryllis Surprises Me Again"

Baltimore Review: "The Home Front" (published as "The Home Front, 1992")

Beloit Poetry Journal: "Cherries"

Blackbox Manifold: "Everywhere and Nowhere at the Same Time," "Fever," and "The Coming World"

Crab Creek Review: "Alphaville," "Hard Candy," and "The Slow Alphabet of Rain"

Cumberland River Review: "Aubade for the City that Never Sleeps," and "Dawn Chorus"

Diode: "Aubade for Losing" (published as "Aubade for Pain")

Dos Gatos Press (anthology *Notes of Light and Dark: Southwestern Aubades and Nocturnes*, 2025): "August," "How We Live," and "Wintering"

Dunes Review: "August"

In Parentheses Magazine: "Unrequited"

Jet Fuel Review: "Lontaine"

Lily Poetry Review: "Letter in Spring"

McNay Museum (commissioned work): "End of Day, 'Nightscape V.' by Louise Nevelson"

Newfound Poetry: "Elegy for Avenue B"

Nine Mile Magazine: "Afterlife"

Ploughshares: "Solstice" (published as "October")

Poet Lore: "Season" (published as "Living On")
Press 52: "Elegy for Orion"
Quiet Lightning: "Medea Talks About Our Stars"
Red Mare Press (handmade chapbook, 2023): "Medea by the
    Water's Edge"
Red Rock Review: "Aubade for Inordinate Love"
Rock Paper Poem: "Walking the Neighborhood"
Rougarou: "Arroyo Seco"
Rubbertop Review: "Hurt Magic"
South Carolina Review: "Heartbreak"
Third Point Press: "Amaryllidaceae"
Tinderbox Review: "Recovery"
West Trade Review: "A list of what I cannot touch"

"Elegy for Avenue B," "Lontaine," "Amaryllidaceae," "Everywhere and Nowhere at the Same Time," "The Earth," "Letter in Spring," "Dawn Chorus," and "Medea Talks About Our Stars," appeared in a chapbook *For the Loneliness of Walking Out* from Lily Poetry Review Books.

This book was written with the support of the Hosking Houses Trust, 33 Duck Lane, The Square, Stradford-upon-Avon, Warwickshire CV37, UK. I want to profoundly thank Sarah Hosking for her warmth, friendship and her brave and steadfast support of women writers and artists over forty.

Thank you to my poetry friends Jennifer Bartlett, Elena Karina Byrne, Lauren Camp, Lois P. Jones, Tami Haaland, Melissa Kwasny, Susan Nguyen, Octavio Quintanilla, Natalia Treviño, Viktoria Valenzuela, Alexandra van de Kamp, Connie Voisine, and Joni Wallace for their—invaluable!—support and advice in the making of these poems. A heartfelt thanks also to Laura Van Prooyen whose astute editorial eye has meant the world. I am so fortunate to be published by Next Page Press!

And to my family—Duncan, Annabelle, Walker, Eliza whose love lights each day.

About the Author

Sheila Black is the author of five poetry collections, most recently *Radium Dream*, (Salmon Poetry, 2022) and four chapbooks, including *For the Loneliness of Walking Out* (Lily Review Poetry Books, 2025). Poems and essays have appeared in *Kenyon Review Online*, *Crab Creek Review*, *The Nation*, *The New York Times*, and elsewhere. She is a co-editor of *Beauty is a Verb: The*  *New Poetry of Disability* (Cinco Puntos Press, 2011), and a 2012 Witter Bynner Fellow with the Library of Congress, for which she was selected by Philip Levine.